# BEHAVIOUR LANGUAGE SCRIPTS FOR TEACHERS

## Tony Curtis

*2nd Edition*

1

# CONTENTS

What the book is about ........................................................................6

Ethics .......................................................................................................8

How to use the book ............................................................................11

The study ..............................................................................................13

Brain functions ....................................................................................15

The list ..................................................................................................23

Brain and perception .........................................................................25

Brain and language ............................................................................32

Memes ...................................................................................................33

Memes and language .........................................................................36

Hypnosis, Neuro-linguistic Programming and Suggestion..........38

Understanding language effects ......................................................41

How to write a script ..........................................................................49

    Script Sheet...................................................................................53

    Script Sheet – Example ..............................................................54

Scripts....................................................................................................55

Mix and match language bank..........................................................56

    Presuppositions ...........................................................................56

    Pacing and Leading.....................................................................57

    Anchors..........................................................................................58

    Primes and triggers.....................................................................59

    Frames ...........................................................................................60

    Binds and double binds .............................................................61

    Deepening......................................................................................62

    Language Plan ..............................................................................63

    Language Plan – Example 1 .......................................................64

    Language Plan – Example 2.......................................................65

Create your own meme..................................................................66

    Meme Plan – Trojan Horse ...............................................67

    Meme plan – Trojan Horse ...............................................68

    Meme Plan – Repetition.....................................................69

    Meme Plan – Repetition Example ....................................70

    Meme Plan – Cognitive Dissonance ................................71

    Meme Plan – Cognitive Dissonance Example.................72

Memetics conclusion.......................................................................73

About the Author.............................................................................74

Image and Book references & Further Reading.........................75

# WHAT THE BOOK IS ABOUT

A well-known communication principle states that, 'You cannot *not* communicate.' Even when you are not speaking, your silence and body language communicates something. Similarly, when you talk, the whole purpose is to translate the ideas and images from your mind into those who are listening with as little break down in fidelity as possible. But how people interpret the words they are hearing in their own minds is often beyond your control. Indeed, you only need to remember a miscommunication or misunderstanding from your own life to see how easy mistakes can be made when you think you have spoken so clearly. Understanding words, how they are represented in the mind and especially how they affect behaviour is at the heart of this book.

All communication has the potential to change a person's emotional state because words carry with them meaning and triggers that have been learnt and embedded over a lifetime of use and experience. Some words carry a universal meaning and are strong enough to grab attention such as, *fire, help, murder or duck!* You will notice that all of these words are involved in danger in some way; that is not by accident. We tend to instinctively react to words that could mean the difference between life and death for obvious reasons. Yet each person carries with them their own unique experience that also produces important words that have meaning and are triggers for them such as their name, names of their children and anything that has been given enough emotional attachment to be placed on the list (we'll discuss the list later in the book)! However, due to globalisation of cultures, societal norms and language, spread through media such as movies and music, these experiences are more accessible and understandable than ever before. By having these experiences, and so the words and triggers associated, more to hand, we can use them to alter a person's emotional state.

No matter what we are doing, we are always in an emotional state, or a mix of states, which can be influenced by the communication and triggers we receive. Once you understand the power of the language you use and how you can structure your communication to elicit the responses you want from others', you will be amazed at what you can accomplish. How can you move a person from a negative state to a positive state? How can you increase the likelihood of a person being in a positive state and therefore more likely to react in a positive way? These questions will also be looked at in this book, the content of which has been put together from over twenty-five years of experience and research in schools and specialist behavioural establishments across the UK. It is hoped that it can offer teachers and support staff working with students, the language skills needed to minimise negative interactions that will naturally increase the potential on task time and positive teacher/student relationship to increase the student's self-esteem, which will then lead naturally to higher attainment and better outcomes.

In the current educational climate of creating a 21st Century School, along with its new buildings and facilities, an ever-evolving model of excellence and teaching practice has led to an influx of strategies to eliminate disruptions in the classroom. Many of these tend to focus on mobile phone use, wearing of uniform in the 'correct' way and the use of stricter and stricter behaviour policies and consequences.

The need to reduce disruption is obviously a good thing; to maximise the learning time a student has in each lesson, to minimise negative behavioural issues which can potentially lead to disaffection, and improving the opportunities available to students by helping them gain higher grades. Some of the classroom strategies used and taught to accomplish this over the years include the use of tonal range in a teacher's voice (Martin & Darnley. 2004), the use of specific body language by a teacher (Neill & Caswell, 2005) and the use of music to guide students' behaviour in a classroom (Fontana, 1985). What these strategies have in common is that they acknowledge that a teacher has a substantial influence on the students' behaviour and that a teacher could and should use that influence for the purpose of positive control.

This book is about the use of specific language and how it can be used to motivate and encourage the behaviour you want to see in your classroom/school/students. The book draws from a wide range of research and knowledge including that of neuro-linguistic programming, suggestion, hypnosis language patterns, neuroscience and specific educational research that has been carried out.

The research into these techniques within a classroom has shown that the language scripts and the increased knowledge that this book provides, could easily be implemented into a teacher's classroom management routine and within a school's behaviour management policy without disruption. If the scripts and language techniques are to be used within a school, this book offers comprehensive training on their use and awareness of the ethical issues associated.

# ETHICS

Every school is interested in minimising the number of negative behavioural responses from its students and increasing on task time. Some of the initiatives brought into schools by the Local Authorities (LA), Academy chains and Head-teachers include painting classrooms different colours to affect students' attitudes, behaviours and learning (Sinofsky and Knirck, 1981); the introduction of Social, Emotional Aspects of Learning (SEAL) which aim to help students learn the skills they need in order to behave well (DSCF 2005) and the theory of multiple intelligences (auditory, kinaesthetic etc.) and their use in creating input stimulus best suited to each 'type' of learner and the use of teachers' voice, posture and body language in classroom management (Gardner 2005), and a 'zero tolerance' approach to behaviour management.

Sinofsky and Knirck (1981) found that colour influences student attitudes, behaviours and learning. In fact, they cited important reasons for using colour effectively in learning environments including the theory that colour affects a student's attention span and affects the student's and teacher's sense of time. Papadatos (1973) suggested that the proper use of colour in schools can convert an atmosphere that is depressing and monotonous into one that is pleasing, exciting and stimulating. He concluded that such change in colour schemes in schools would reduce absenteeism and promote positive feelings about school.

The aim of the SEAL programme is to ensure that schools have the skills and support they need in order to maintain a creative and positive learning environment for all pupils. It is also aimed at helping schools promote positive behaviour for learning and tackle the issue of low-level disruption (DCSF). The visual, auditory, read/write and kinaesthetic (VARK) guide to learning styles, devised by Fleming and Mills in 1992, consists of four preferred ways of receiving information - visual, aural, reading/writing and kinaesthetic. This is one of the most common and widely-used categorizations of the various types of learning styles and Fleming's VARK model which expanded on the model of neuro-linguistic programming (NLP), is used by more and more schools (Morgan, 2009).

The use of zero tolerance behaviour, which some teaching unions have called 'inhumane' (The Guardian 2009), use extremely strict criteria for punishing

8

students within a school setting. Indeed. Not only are the criteria for punishment very tight, but so too in the punishment dealt, with increasing use of isolation rooms and exclusions that could potentially be damaging to students' mental health.

The modification of language to influence behaviour has already been established in schools with the use of common terms and phrases standard so that all students are getting the same message using the same words. Therefore, the addition of a more specific and potentially more powerful method could be included without much deviation from normal practice. And if it improves behaviour and teacher/student relationships without the need for any of the interventions mentioned above, surely that is a good thing?

All of these initiatives have one thing in common; they manipulate the exterior stimulus (colour, language, voice, and environment etc.) in order to produce a change in the behavioural response of the students (often subconsciously). This book follows the same 'stimulus – response' model of classical conditioning (Pavlov, 1927) that the other strategies and programmes followed in that the specific language input taught will impact on the student's behavioural outputs and be embedded in their minds to elicit certain responses. However, instead of the usual classical conditioning model, we will not be pairing unconditional stimuli with conditioned stimuli in order to produce a conditioned response, but we will be using conditioned behaviour responses that already exist in the student, and by changing our own language stimuli, will affect the strength of their specific responses as we desire.

The Behavioural, Emotional and Social Difficulties guidance states that children and young people with behavioural and emotional difficulties should be supported in reaching expectations and participating fully in school. The school should also have in place a system of prevention, early identification and intervention to underpin the key duties set out in the Childcare Act on local authorities and their partners. Paragraph 7:60 of the SEN Code of Practice suggests that children and young people with behaviour and emotional difficulties may require help with acquiring the skills of positive interaction with peers and adults and require specialised behavioural and cognitive approaches.

This book can be used within schools to support students in reaching their expectations and participating fully in lessons. It will also help students improve their relationships with adults in school which can only lead to a more enjoyable environment and deeper learning.

Some may say that this manipulation of a person's predicted future is a form a brainwashing, however the contrary is believed to be the case by most psychologists in this field. The minds' ability to predict the future show that humans are no longer stimulus driver because their internal models of the future are so well developed. Using the posterior parietal cortex which is linked to the prefrontal cortex gives the human the power to stop and think which is at the heart of our power to resist brainwashing (Taylor, 2004).

This book is not the first to use suggestion to influence teaching in a classroom. The Bulgarian psychotherapist Georgi Lazanov created a method called Suggestopedia (Lazanov, 1978) which used music, modified texts and tone of voice to enhance the learning of students. Lozanov suggested that his method was a system for liberation from the negative concepts and difficulties of the learning process.

This idea of a technique liberating and freeing students is also reflected in a paper by Dr Ralph Dale (Dale, 1972, MacMillan 1988, Astor 1971) in which he suggests that hypnosis in education should be orientated toward the student having the option and power to use auto-suggestion. This means that the students themselves have the knowledge to self-induce a hypnotic state to aid learning and control negative behaviour and will therefore have all the power of choice.

This is a more empowering idea than using the script alone, however, it relies on the students knowing when to apply it and being able to use it in a potentially emotionally charged situation. An example of this would be the 'reflective planner' and the 'automatic doer' of Richard Thaler and Cass Sunstein's 'Temptation and Mindlessness' (Thaler & Sunstein, 2009). They suggest that during our 'cold' state of mind, our brains can plan events and decisions reflectively with their own interest at heart; to eat healthily for example. Yet, when we become aroused we enter a 'hot' state in which we can act automatically and behave contrary to our plans. An example of this could be a delicious smell of fried food or the sight of chocolate making you break your self-imposed diet. They describe this as being dynamically inconsistent. It is, therefore, not the safest of options to leave the interventions solely in the hands of the benefactors.

# HOW TO USE THE BOOK

This book is split into two parts. The first part gives you the knowledge and information on the brain and which parts are associated with the work we will be focusing on; the language patterns that will be used, how they are structured and what they accomplish; and also the associated research with each relevant discipline. The second part teaches you how to use this information to structure and build your own scripts for a variety of purposes. This section can be photocopied and shared as much as you need. Some schools and departments have kept a bank of scripts that have been particularly potent.

Follow these simple steps to make the most out of the book:

- Learn and understand the language types

There are many different types of language that can be used on their own or in conjunction with each other to aid behaviour management. The definitions of them are found in the 'understanding language effects' section with examples for you to use in the 'mix & match language bank'. Learn, understand and read around the subject using the 'references and further reading' list.

- Do the mini exercises

There are examples of all the language types and their uses throughout this book. Get into the habit of practicing them yourself and look for examples where they are already happening. The mini exercises are designed to show you how the language scripts work and help you make your own.
- Put together some scripts to try

Using the 'mix & match language bank' and the blank script sheets, you can begin to write your own language scripts to elicit the behaviour responses you want. It is important to add to the language bank with your own versions of words that work best with your vocabulary and for your students. That way the scripts are in your style and not forced and will be adapted for the students in front of you.


- Keep a diary on your progress

There are several sections at the bottom of each script sheet for you to review how the script is going. This is an important feature of building your own scripts so that you can continue to improve them. It is good practice to review your script for each group you are using it with as each group's reaction will be slightly different.

– Adapt and keep trying

By using the information in this book including the language descriptors, the language bank, script sheets and resources, you will be able to build and design your own scripts to use. The more you use and review the scripts the better you will become at adapting them for the different audiences you will face. Keep working on them and improving your use of them and you will see a marked improvement without doubt.

# THE STUDY

In 2010, after 17 years of working in schools focusing on behaviour, I began a research project to establish whether the specific language a teacher used in a classroom could have a positive effect on the behaviour and response of their students. By analysing neuro-linguistic programming, hypnosis induction scripts, influence and persuasion techniques and the neuroscience of language I took elements from each that complemented each other and created scripts that I thought would positively influence the behaviour of students.

I purposely created classes that would be used to test these ideas that were filled with students who were at risk of exclusion due to behaviour difficulties.

The first script I wrote was designed to get their attention in the class whenever I wanted it. As you can imagine, with a class full of students with behaviour issues, getting all of their attention at the same time is problematic. The first few weeks of gaining a baseline without using the script was very difficult. On average it took over six minutes to get them to focus on me when I wanted them to.

Then followed weeks of testing using the first script. Initially, speaking the script as a whole, which then reduced down to just using a prime and a trigger. It resulted in a reduction time of 93% in getting students' attention. In real terms that meant that it went from over six minutes to just 9 seconds.

The scripts were then analysed, changed and tested again resulting in a reduction of 97% in the time required to gain the students' attention. This meant that it went from over 6 minutes before the script to just 4 seconds using the script.

What is important to note is that after the first few lessons using the script in full, later lessons only used the 'prime' and 'trigger' to activate the desired response. The 'prime' in this case was a hand clap, and the 'trigger' was the word listen.

The scripts were then taught to other teachers to use with their classes of different year groups and subjects. All reported a significant reduction in response time from their classes to around 4 seconds.

One interesting result in my research showed that the majority of students do not even notice anything out of the ordinary during the use of tailored language scripts.

In fact, even those students who were already showing the behaviour I was trying to elicit (focused on me and listening) had no awareness that a script was being used.

This is a good indication that the scripts do not register in the students' consciousness enough to be a detriment to their learning or to raise concern. This is a key point and shows that this book remains within the ethical guidelines established with the DfE and that it could be incorporated into a classroom management plan without disruption to the teaching or to the students' awareness.

My research into language stimulus and behaviour response showed that using tailored language scripts utilised in established models such as neuro-linguistic programming, hypnosis induction scripts, suggestibility and neuroscience can positively affect the behaviour responses from students which in turn increases each lesson's potential learning time and decrease negative behavioural instances. I have trained staff in mainstream settings and specialist schools in using these scripts and am now sharing it with you.

# BRAIN FUNCTIONS

Some basic knowledge of brain function in regard to behaviour and language is interesting to note but not essential to being able to learn and adapt the language scripts taught in this book. What this book offers is by no means a comprehensive insight on the subject and you are encouraged to read more using the references and further reading lists at the end of the book.

When an input stimulus is received by the brain from any of the senses seeing, hearing feeling something etc.), it passes the information around the brain via neurons (see image below). When an axon is stimulated to release a neurotransmitter across the synapse it travels to a receptor on the opposing dendrite, altering both cells in the process. The bombardment of transmitter molecules across the same neurons can cause long lasting changes in the cell's electrical status, the genetic machinery which can produce more transmitter and receptors, which will make activation of the synapse much more sensitive and thus easier to reproduce. This is a technical way of saying that the more someone uses certain neurons for speaking, visualizing, behaviour or memory, the more likely they are to be repeated in the future with a much lower tolerance for activation.

This is how learning happens, commonly used neurons can be activated much easier than those occasionally used; the more frequent and intense the incoming signal is to the neurons, the stronger the neurons and their links will become (Britannia 2008, Greenfield, 2008). Conversely, retiring and little used axons and dendrites will be much harder to stimulate and may even be cut altogether. The more frequent and intense the incoming signal is to some neurons the stronger those neural links will become. This is why repetition is an important feature in learning and why changing learned behaviour can be difficult and time consuming.

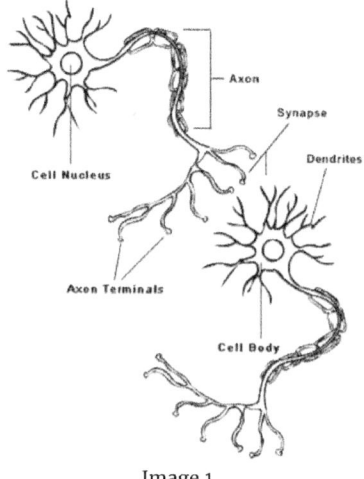

Image 1

In Kathleen Taylor's 2004 book Brainwashing: The Science of Thought Control, she compares the strength of behaviour patterns to the size of pipes used to transfer water. Imagine a reservoir which has been filled with water and which there are multiple exit channels in the form of different sized pipes. If one of the pipes is narrow and another is wider, water will naturally flow faster through the channel that is wider. Channels in the water-flow metaphor correspond to cognitive networks with the channel size to neural strength and the water, to an input signal. As water flows, it wears away obstacles, creating a smoother flow and larger channels. The equivalent is true for neural activity. Neurons activated at the same time over and over again change the synapses between them so that signals flow easier and much smoother from input to output. This is an important piece of information if we are to change the responses to stimuli and control the shape the behaviour outputs of our students.

Once you replace the analogy of water with information or neuronal activity and the pipes with the neurons themselves carrying this information, you can see that the scripts you use have the ability to change the pathways and sensitivity of particular behaviours within the brain which will allow responses to be made stronger and easier. The length of retention of the scripts and their associated behaviours are reduced if the scripts are not used regularly as other more important synaptic links would be created during this time, weakening those of the scripts. Therefore, it is important that once you start using the scripts, you can then use the 'primer' and 'trigger' alone after a while to elicit the response, but it is always good practice to use the full script every so often to keep the connections strong.

16

Behaviour is a fluid function that can be switched and changed rapidly. We all have different personae which we adopt in different social situations that have been learned and adapted throughout our lives. These personae, usually referred to as 'roles' or 'schemas' in neuro-linguistic programming, include set behaviours, thoughts, attitudes, feelings and language that the brain uses in different social settings. In new situations, your brain will try to find a relevant behaviour pattern for you to adopt in order for you to fit in (and stay alive).

Consider this; try to remember the last time you were on a night out with your friends with a few drinks and familiar company. Think about the language you used, the behaviour you displayed and the jokes you told. Sounds like a great night! Now try to remember a visit you had to an elderly relative. Compare the behaviour, language and conversation you would have in one situation compared to the other. You may think this obvious, but when you examine it, you have the ability to modify your outward behaviour whilst keeping your internal self the same, and you did it without having to consciously make the change. It just happens naturally right?

So let's say for some reason you were invited to visit the queen; which behaviour pattern would you most likely adopt? Although you probably have never met the queen before, your mind would find the most suitable schema you have and use the prefrontal cortex to stay hyper vigilant throughout your visit. By the time you leave you would have created a whole new 'visit the queen' set of behaviours (as well as gained a massive headache from the resources needed to maintain that amount of focus). Don't worry, the next time you visit, the behaviour will kick in naturally and you will be more relaxed.

When doing new and challenging tasks, the pre-frontal cortex is primarily responsible for figuring out what is going on. If the task is quite intense or long lasting you will start to get a headache in this area from overuse. As these tasks become familiar with repetition, the pre-frontal cortex will become less and less involved in their activation. Due to the huge amount of energy required to power the pre-frontal cortex, the brain attempts to conserve its use wherever possible. Instead, the attention required is moved to other parts of the brain, such as the posterior parietal cortex, which uses significantly less energy.

The reason why the posterior parietal cortex and such regions use much less energy than the prefrontal cortex is because they use generalities, rules of thumb and easy neural pathways to perform most of its tasks rather than concentrating on the finer details.

These learned patterns of thought and behaviours are the 'paths of least resistance' in the brain, meaning that they are used more often, they are easier to trigger and that they have, more or less, kept the person safe by using them. The three main factors that determine the strength of the set pattern of behaviour are:

- The timings of the neural inputs (close to the input trigger)
- The frequency of the inputs (neurons that fire together, wire together)
- Their significance to the person (how emotionally charged they are)

This is important when beginning to understand why people act and react in certain situations and why it is easier to change some people's behaviour than others. We will be purposely changing the strength of some of the neural pathways that lead to the behaviour patterns we want to elicit in certain situations around the school.

Another way the brain conserves energy is with the use of predictions. Humans are constantly making predictions about the world around them. They derive them from expectations of how the world is likely to be in the near future and previous experience that has built their mental world and in part from what their actions have achieved in the past. Why do you start singing the next song on an album just as the previous song ends? Your successful predictions are associated with the subjective experience of a smooth stream of consciousness that is only broken when the predictions fail. Have you ever taken an extra step on the stairs when you thought there was one more to go? Organisms that are able to predict the future (based on past experience) are no longer purely stimulus driven as their internal models of the future become more likely to influence behaviour. However, in younger, less educated or less experienced brains, the balance between incoming information and information stored in memory gives greater weight to the incoming information as the person has less historical data to draw from. He or she is therefore more likely to be stimulus driven, reacting to the immediate environment rather than stopping to think about past consequences.

Image 2

Take this picture (above) for instance. You know what it is lurking in the grass right? Ok, so describe a lion for me in your mind right now. A quick list may go something like:

- A main of hair around its head
- Two eyes
- Two ears
- A nose a mouth
- A body
- Four legs
- A tail

You probably got something similar. Okay, now look at the picture again. How many legs can you see? How many tails? How many bodies? How many items on the checklist can you actually see? Not that many right? Yet you still know it's a lion and if you say that walking towards you, you wouldn't wait until the last item is checked off before you knew it was a lion before you ran. You would predict, with as little information as possible, what the thing is and if it was a danger to you so that you can run that much sooner and stay alive.

Granted, we don't see many lions walking around the streets these days, but that doesn't stop the mind from analysing the incoming data in order to predict what things are and what dangers they might possess.

What does this mean for students within your class setting? It means that they will predict the future of your lessons based on previous experience (and bad experiences register more deeply) but they are still able to be stimulated in order to change that perception. Here is an example. Think back to when you were at school, was there a particular teacher you hated? There is often one for most people that, for whatever reason, didn't seem to like them. If I were to take you back into that class, with its decor and its smell, your mind would instantly and uncontrollably be thrown back to when you were a child and create the same feelings and memories of before. You may even remember specific events that were traumatic which would make you feel a bad, just as you did back then.

The input stimulus of approaching the room, the sights inside, the smell all trigger a memory of past events in this space and bring about the emotions associated with it in order to let you know in no uncertain circumstances, that this place is not good for them. How much learning do you think you could do in this place with those emotions running through you?

So now that you are in control of your classroom experience and that of your students, how do they predict the next lesson will go and how will that effect their emotions? I'm not saying that it is your fault that a student behaves a certain way, So many times the triggers for their emotional state have fired way before they even step into your room. What I am saying is that once they have, you have the power to set up and fire off different triggers, ones that will have a positive effect and will naturally change their prediction of the next lesson with you.

Now an interesting thing happens when a prediction is shown to not be coming true in the mind. For starters, the mind, like most of us, doesn't like to be wrong, and when it's finding out that it may be, it cheats in order to be right. When a prediction is made that is not or has not come true it creates a gap between the two called a cognitive dissonance. This gap can be quite painful for the mind and it will try different things in order to close it. It will motivate you to behave in a certain way that will make the prediction come true. It will insert a reason (quite often bizarre) for the prediction not coming true. And in rare cases, it will even go against everything that it has previously known and knows to be true.

For example, a student who has been having a bad time in a class recently, walks towards the room again for their next lesson. The mind remembers the last few lessons and how it made them feel and makes a prediction that it will be another bad lesson and they are likely to be kicked out again. They go in and sit down. They are given some work that they can do and they start working on it. After a while of having a pretty good lesson, the mind will say, 'hold on. I predicted that it will be a bad lesson, what's going on?' It will then seek to make its prediction correct by placing things on 'the list' that will draw their attention. 'Is that kid looking at me? Who's making that noise that's so annoying? I wonder what's going on out of the window. All of which are easy to elicit as they are behaviours that are used daily. It sets up a cognitive ease, when something is familiar, feels true, feels good and feels effortless, to close the gap. Now the teacher may say something to them about staying on task which would elicit a much bigger response from the student than deserved. So it escalates the situation, the lesson turns out bad and they get thrown out and although it may seem like a negative thing from the teacher's point of view (and will be for the student overall), right then, the gap is filled, the prediction is held up and all is right with the world. There is a sense of ease in the mind and the pain of getting it wrong is gone.

If you were to ask the student (which I have done), what was that all about. They will usually find reasons why they acted the way they did. What's his name was looking at me funny, I heard someone say my name, the teacher hates me, I did nothing etc; all to fill the gap and make the world a safe and predictable place once again.

You have probably filled the gap in the same way many times. Displayed behaviour that you can't really explain, or came up with an implausible excuse when something hasn't gone as predicted (adding an extra step you try to walk up on the stairs – 'why took that step away?')

There have been moments of tragedy that create such a gap that the mental and physical pain is just too much to cope and the mind will create any reason not to know the real reason it exists. Take for example a true case of a mother who, one morning, sends her child off to school with a packed lunch and a kiss on the forehead as always. The mind predicting that it will be a regular Tuesday like any other and later that day the child will return and still not clean their bedroom. On the way to school however, the child is hit by a car and killed. When the mother is told about what has happened, the cognitive dissonance created between the prediction and the reality is so painful that the mind simply refuses to believe it. She says things like, 'they are at school but have been kept behind', or 'they are going round a friend's house after school' so won't be home. All of which is complete nonsense, but much easier and less painful that acknowledging the gap.

There are some behaviours however, that are shared between students and seem to be passed unconsciously between them (take for example the wearing of shirts that are untucked)! You may recognize this in the actions and reactions of students of different ages to those around them. During a child's early years, the experiences they have and the feedback they get will start to set their behaviours and ideas within the neural pathways of their mind. However, the importance placed on ideas changes over time as pressure to conform to a group emerges (to fit in with the 'cool' kids and not to stand out. This is a subconscious decision to prevent aggression and rejection). There is a relatively new and very interesting scientific area which is beginning to understand the use of and transport of these ideas in a person, called memetics. A meme is a piece of information that can be passed from one person to another (now taken on a whole new meaning thanks to social media). Similar to a gene that can pass genetic information from parent to child (vertically), a meme passes a thought or idea from person to person (horizontally) and as such can travel much more rapidly. You will have seen how fast memes can spread with a few examples. Remember Pokémon? How quickly those little cards spread from the Far East across the world. And the perceived value of those 'rare' cards made collectors out of young and old alike. Music, fashion, sayings and beliefs spread across the young minds faster than wildfire and often go as quickly as they come. Think 'fidget-spinners' for a second!

This area of study can also be used to create a new idea or behaviour set for your classroom and school. There is more information on memes and memetics in a later chapter.

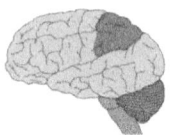 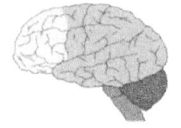 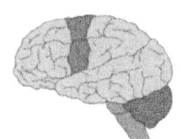 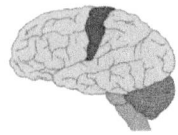

| Posterior Parietal Cortex | Prefrontal Cortex | Motor Cortex | Somatosensory Cortex |

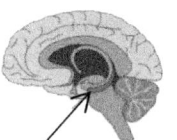 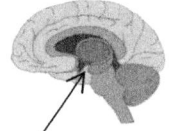 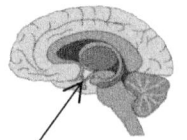 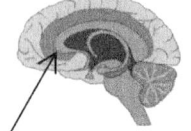

| Hippocampus | Amygdala | Hypothalamus | Anterior Cingulate Gyrus |

Image 3

# THE LIST

I've mentioned 'the list' a few times now so I had better explain what it is. The list is a series of things that are important enough to gain your attention and direct your focus, over and above the noise of all incoming signals. The list is held in the anterior cingulate gyrus, and acts like a secretary to the big boss. Making him aware of all the important bits of information and keeping the not so important out.

Items on the list are a mix of fairly universal things, some things that are personal to you and some temporary things you put on the list just for a short while.

Examples of things on the list that are fairly generic are mostly based on things that are dangerous. The word danger, warning, knife, murder, all pique our interest and cause us to be aware of our surroundings. This is not surprising considering our need for survival. However, if these things are overused and cause you to question if there is actual danger at all they become demoted. How many red speed signs do you pass while still going over the limit?

Personal items on the list are put on through years of experience. Your name is a common one. Have you ever been in a crowded, noisy room, when out of nowhere you hear your name being said? It isn't because someone said it louder than everything else. It is because your secretary was keeping a track on everything that was going on and being said and your name was important enough to pass on to the boss.

Now items that you put on the temporary list are important to you for a short while. A little while ago I was in the market for a new car. I quite liked the look of the new mini so decided to go to a garage on the weekend and have a look at them. The next morning I woke up and went to work as normal when all of a sudden, there were mini's everywhere! I saw them on the roads, I saw them in driveways, I even saw them on billboard posters that I hadn't noticed before. Now, everyone didn't go out that night and buy a mini and the poster wasn't put up just for me. Mini's had suddenly become important to be and so my secretary made me aware of every one that was around.

For temporary things on the list to be made more permanent, it needs something a little extra for it to qualify. That is, emotion. The Anterior Cingulate Gyrus is located near an area called the limbic system that contains the hypothalamus, Amygdala and the Hippocampus. These three play a crucial role in assigning emotion to events and memories and their functions are:

**Amygdala** – giving meaning to emotions, remembered, and attached to associations and responses to them (emotional memories).

**Hippocampus** - storing of long-term memory, which includes all past knowledge and experiences.

**Hypothalamus** – regulating emotional responses

So you can see that things that want to pass from the temporary list to the permanent one need to be associated with a strong emotion (as close to the event at possible), that is then more likely to be stored in the long term memory so that when they are seen or occur again can be responded to and brought to our attention and perceived.

# BRAIN AND PERCEPTION

Now you think that once something is perceived then it's all good. Well, I'm sorry to disappoint you. Perception is a complex set of actions that bring together all the input channels (sight, hearing etc.), cross references them with previous memories and emotions and then double checks to make sure that it fits in with whatever predictions are made.

This means that the world you perceive around you isn't really the world as it is. It is merely your brains interpretation of what the world is and if something doesn't fit within this world, then it may not be perceived at all or even perceived as something completely different.

Take the image below for example. This is called the Necker Cube first published 1832 by Swiss crystallographer Louis Albert Necker. You'll see eight dots with what appears to be the corner of a cube in each one. You can see the cube pretty easily and if you look closer, you may even be able to see a brighter white of the cube's lines between each dot.

Image 4

What is shown is simply eight dots with pieces cut out of it. It is your mind that creates the image of the cube and even adds more detail that isn't there, such as the imaginary 'whiter' lines that join them. The mind does this because it has to quickly make sense of limited data and represent it in a meaningful way (remember the partial lion). It takes what it thinks should be there and makes you see that, whether it's there or not.

Look at the next picture. You will see and image of a checkerboard with a cylinder in one corner. You will see tile A and tile B. What can you tell me about them? They appear to be different shades of grey right?

Image 5

26

They are actually the same shade of grey. Even with the helpful block below showing them the same, your mind will, even now, try to change the shade of the grey as you move your eyes from A to B.

Image 6

I know you probably won't believe me so see for yourself. Try and cover everything but the tiles and you will see that they are all indeed the same grey.

Now what is going on here? Even knowing that they are the same grey doesn't change the fact that they still appear either lighter or darker to you. That is because your mind is looking at the picture and saying, 'yep, I know what this is. It looks like a chess board with black and white tiles, I've seen them a thousand times so therefore I don't have to look at them again for you to see them. So your mind projects what it 'thinks' should be there, not what is actually there. The fact that the tiles aren't those shades makes no difference at all. Your mind expects to see those shades so that's what you see.

Now that example is on a simple flat, stationary image. What do you think happens with the chaotic moving images that pass in front of your eyes every day? Exactly the same thing but most of the time you would be unaware of any mistakes as they simply wouldn't matter. It is only when they cause a mistake that you become aware of that you realise something isn't quite right.

Again, using the prediction based system of the mind, it tries to organise and classify every piece of information it receives as best it can. If you actually saw, heard, felt everything in detail, you would need to use an enormous amount of processing power to analyse, make use of and store the incoming information which would make the brain an organ that simply uses too much energy to be viable. How the mind gets around this though is by pretending that everything is at it should be whilst using shortcuts, quick answers and easy behaviours to paint the world as it thinks it should be so that it looks like a seamless narrative playing out in front of you in an otherwise complicated world.

Take vision for example. Humans are mostly visual creatures. We get through life by seeing what's around us, and using our eyes for pretty much everything we do. So try this, find a spot on the wall in front of you and with your hands outstretched to the sides, slowly bring them in until you can see them out of the corners of your eyes. Pretty wide! Now do the same with the top and the bottom. So you can see a pretty big picture in front of you right? Wrong. What you can actually see in any detail is about the size of your thumbnail at arm's length. This area in the eye is called the Fovea and is the high definition space where you actually see things. It is a tiny pit located in the macula of the retina where its layers are spread aside to let light fall directly onto the cones.

Outside of this you know it as your peripheral vision, which collects only minimal data that is not used for much processing. What this means is that the view of what you see in front of you is mostly made up in the mind based on what it remembers was there and what it thinks should be there and not necessarily what is there to give you a sense of continuity.

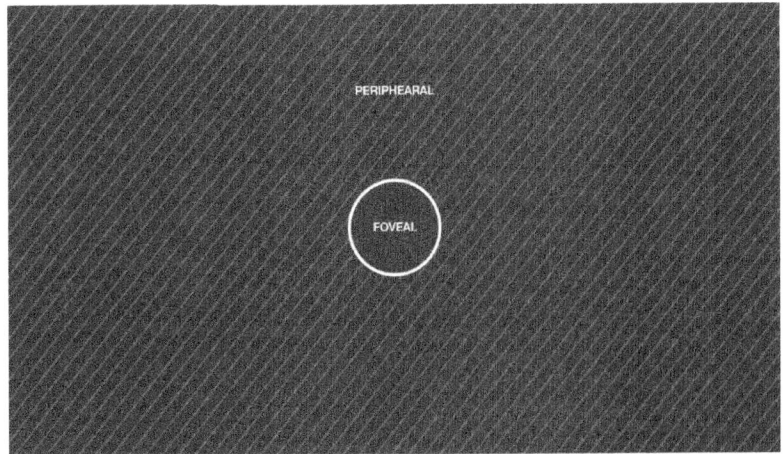

Image 7

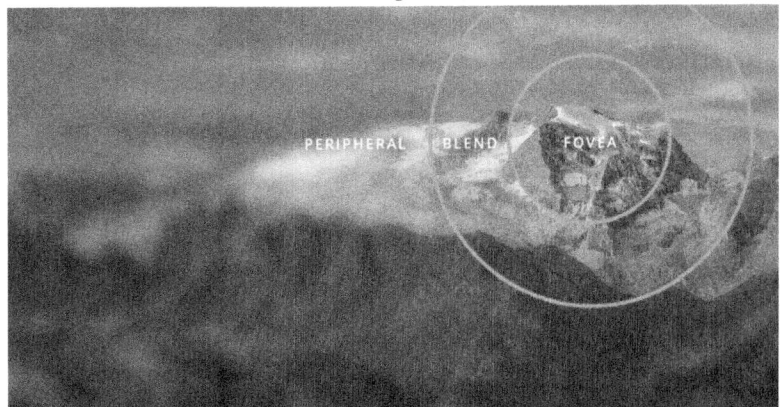

Image 8

There are several experiments that can prove this to you. One of which is called the Flicker Paradigm, which you can Google and see examples of on YouTube. This shows two images being flashed up; Picture A and Picture B. Both look identical but there is something different between them. It's like a flashing spot the difference. What you'll notice is that you won't easily be able to see the difference (if you spot it at all) between them because you cannot see the picture as a whole, even though it's relatively small. However, what is more interesting to note is what your eyes are doing while it is searching for the difference. It is scanning around the image using about the size of your thumbnail trying to spot it.

Another easy way to see this is by staring at a blank area on a wall and then try to read any text that is in front of you but not directly in your line of sight. You can't right. You know the text is there but it's just too blurry to make out.

Another trick the body uses in order to take in as much visual information as possible is by making your eyes flicker. Look at the image below

Image 9

What you will probably notice is that the swirls look like they're rotating, yet when you move your eyes to look at one of the dots in the centre of a moving one it stops. How does it know you're looking at it?

It doesn't of course. What this illusion demonstrates is that your eyes are constantly flickering. It does this by adopting a completely opposite way of using muscles to the rest of your body. If your arm is at rest and you wanted to move it your muscle would have to be activated for it to be set in motion. If you wanted to move it back then the muscle on the opposite side would have to be activated. The same works for your legs, toes, fingers etc. Not so for your eyes. The muscles that are attached to

30

your eyes are constantly activated, which means that they are pulling in all their directions at once. So in order for your eyes to move left, the muscles on the right have to relax (instead of the muscle on the left having to pull). This creates a flickering in the eyes as it tries to maintain equilibrium. It would be like trying to make you arm at rest by activating both the bicep and tricep at the same time and keeping the amount of pull on each the same.

What this all means is that your world and the world of your students is built from small pieces of information that goes to build a model of reality based on memory and prediction. Once you know this, you can begin to it in order to create a new perception and therefore the behaviours that follow.

# BRAIN AND LANGUAGE

The part of the brain most relevant for language is the cerebral cortex. This has been shown by neurological observations; in particular the impact of lesions in certain areas of the cortex has that lead to neurological language impairment and aphasia (Pulvermuller 2002). From a personal perspective, I know the effects that this can have on a person. In 2010 my mother suffered an aneurism in an area that affects speech and language. Following a surgical procedure to repair the damage, she was left without the ability to forms words and sentences in any meaningful order. I spent over a year working with her to learn how to speak again and to adapt the internal processes of what she wanted to say into meaningful speech. It was quite curious and often very funny to see the way her brain would wrongly assign words and meanings to the speech that came out of her mouth. By working with her in reassigning the meaning of words and their correct usage, I was able to see first-hand how the brain and language are connected.

The research into language, the brain and behaviour has helped shape this book by bringing together the most significant and effective tools necessary for the script's success. However, you should be mindful that the level of language you use in the scripts you write should also match the age and awareness of the students to be most effective (Gibson 1984). You will know your students and their language levels better than me so you should be prepared to adapt your scripts in order to meet their language input rather than your own.

Some have argued that gender can play a strong role in influence. This may be true in certain circumstances but there is no clear evidence that gender has a strong influence in persuasion at all (Guadango 2009, Cialdini 2007). In fact, with regard to these scripts we are using, we will not be accessing the sections of the brain that are influenced by gender but will be speaking directly to the subconscious.

# MEMES

Memetics is a relatively new branch of science that deals with the passing on and movement of ideas. It was first coined by Richard Dawkins in his book 'The Selfish Gene' (1976) where he relates them to their biological cousins Genes. Genes, as you know, pass genetic information from parent to child in a vertical model, with each generation passing genetic information onto the next. A Meme is much more fluid in that it can not only passes vertically from parent to child in the form of learning social cultures, religious beliefs and expectations, but can also be passed horizontally from one person to another.

The information, instruction, behaviour or idea that passes between one person and another can be done so by language, inventions, imitation, books or music in the form of words, tunes, catch-phrases, fashion and architecture to name but a few.

A good analogy is to consider your brain as a prime piece or advertising space such as a billboard that you pass under every day. The space on that billboard is very desirable but also very limited in size. Ideas become like mini adverts and will compete in order to appear on the billboard, happily covering each other to stay there.

Similarly, the brain has limited space and resources that it can use to hold and manipulate ideas. Some ideas may be very persistent (such as a song going round and round your head when you are trying to sleep), some ideas can be all encompassing (infatuation with the latest fashion trend or playing card game from Japan) and some ideas are very dangerous for the species (celibacy or suicide for instance). The point is that memes spread themselves indiscriminately and do not care if it is useful or not, it just wants its space in your head. A successful meme is one that not only infects your mind and becomes a deep rooted belief but one that also makes you want to spread it on to others.

What is important about this theory of mind is that it explains the physical growth and cognitive function of the brain that began around two and a half million years ago. It can explain why and how ideas are made, spread and infect brains and it can also be used to predict and create behaviour. Under this definition, memes are the internal representations of knowledge that results in outward effects on the world. Therefore, the spread of memes that influence a person's mind is the control and influence of their behaviour. What is disturbing is that memes enter our minds without our permission and become part of our internal programming without us being aware of it.

Memes can also join together to form memeplexes that are much more powerful than single idea on its own. When memes are replicated and shared together, they do a much better job at sticking in our brains than a single meme. This could be down to the fact that together they make up good rules of thumb that can link many pieces of information together without needing the brains processing power to analyse and input every one. If I ask you to think about a certain type of person, say a 'hipster', you instantly get a whole set of memes in one. These probably include, some kind of beard, skinny jeans, trucker hats, longer hair than usual (maybe even a ponytail), brown boots, drink wine and gin and tonic and be into indie music and independent films. All of these memes are packed into a single memeplex.

The majority of memes are in some way associated with others, this is partly due to the memes being used as building blocks of larger ideas than as whole ideas themselves and partly because our brains instinctively want to anchor associated memes together to save effort.

Advertisers have known about memes and memeplexes, at least without having the name attached to it, for a long time and have built some very successful products on the back of them. Let's take a look at one in detail to unpack how they do it.

Let us look at a particular brand of syrup. Let's suppose someone had the idea of adding water and sugar to this syrup to make a soft drink. Now to start, let's show this drink being used by good looking, happy, sexy people on posters to anchor those ideas to the drink. Then tie in some feel good emotions, perhaps of the most popular holiday of the year, Christmas. Match the colour of the drink to the main icon of the holiday (or change the colour of the icon to match your drink) and create songs and images of them together. Next, bring in the younger minds with games and activities themed to the drink, music giveaways and cool adventurous sports. Throw in a whole load of different celebrities shown drinking it as well to capture a wide variety people who are influenced by them and there you have a very powerful memeplex. I probably don't have to tell you the name of this soft drink as I'm sure you know it well.

Memeplexes are also one of the ways that people can become infected, by means of a Trojan Horse. A memeplex that is fronted by a seemingly harmless idea wouldn't necessarily raise your alarm bells. However, once associated memes begin unpacking ideas around the original meme that are dangerous or against your earlier beliefs, what do you do? You could decide to throw away the idea but you may not want to, especially if you have spent time and energy promoting it. You may remember the Jonestown massacre that happened in 1978. A group started out as an innocent collection called The Peoples Temple who taught biblical revival Christianity and socialism in the US. After being criticized in several areas where its branches were located, they decided to move to Guyana where they could be free to live and believe what they wanted. Following the mass migration of its members, more concerns were raised with members being split from families, child protection issues, increased drug use and the power of the leaders being unquestioned. The initial idea of a Christian society began unpacking other ideas of drug use, isolation and complete dominance by the leaders that eventually led to 918 members committing suicide by drinking a cyanide cocktail.

# MEMES AND LANGUAGE

One way that memes can spread is through the form of language, whether it be written, spoken or visual (as in body language). We could take the methods of language and behaviour control described in the 'Understanding language effects' section and break them down into the component memes that make them, but that is beyond the scope of this book. What we can do though is use those language effects to build our own memeplexes for your home, classroom or workplace.

We have already spoken about the Trojan Horse method of infiltrating a person's brain. There are two other ways in which we can do the same. The first is through conditioning and repetition, just like the conditioned response experiments of Pavlov and his dogs. We could anchor a set of behaviour memes to certain input sensations over and over again to enlarge the neural connectors between the input and output channels. Repetition is used in many memes such as learning your times tables or speaking another language. Repetition and practice embeds the memes you want into the brain. Just think about why adverts are used over and over again on multiple TV channels, in multiple formats. To establish and fully embed the meme of their product in your mind it may take you seeing it on TV, hearing it on the radio and seeing the advertising posters on bus stops, magazines and billboards.

The second way to infect a mind is with cognitive dissonance. As we have learned, cognitive dissonance occurs when a new piece of information comes in to the brain which conflicts with an already held idea or prediction. Here's an example. John considers himself a caring and generous man. He shows this in the things he does and the words he uses and people around him agree with him. One day he is confronted by a person wanting him to contribute some of his wages to a local charity. If he refuses, a cognitive dissonance is created between him being a caring person and him not giving to charity. He may reconcile this gap with a self-generated meme that says he is internally happy with what he currently does to support charities and probably makes a list to help himself of all that he does to confirm this. Or he may agree and pay up.

The problem is, the larger the gap between the two ideas, the greater his need will be to fill it. Now, people in John's work have gotten on board with this local charity and have asked John if he is donating (knowing how caring he is). John's cognitive dissonance has now grown beyond the small internal gap of seeing himself as a caring person and has now increased to include his outward appearance to his colleagues. Many psychological studies have shown that people will work to reduce the dissonance between incompatible ideas, so the pressure to pay up increases (or to come up with a bigger internal meme to explain the gap).

This means that if we present a new idea that conflicts with a person's currently held ideas, we set up a cognitive dissonance. If we then offer a meme which alleviates the pain of the gap they are far more likely to take it in and accept it.

# HYPNOSIS, NEURO-LINGUISTIC PROGRAMMING AND SUGGESTION

Although the scripts in this book are not directly using hypnosis, some of you may have been worried or have felt wary when the word was used. There has been a great misrepresentation in the media over hypnosis with stage performers and evil villains employing some of its techniques. But hypnosis is at its heart, a therapeutic tool which helps to bypass the barriers to change that often inhibit progression and change. Many psychologists have used hypnosis in the past with children both in the school setting and outside. With the formation of the British Society of Experimental and Clinical Hypnosis in 1978, hypnosis became freely available to children as a new pool of professionals entered the field including dentists and educational psychologists (Gibson, 1984). As a result, it began being used in schools (Benson 1984) with new ground being made in its use with young people, many of whom were classed as delinquents and placed in local authority care for assessment.

From the work done in this area a fundamental question arose about children with behavioural problems; did the problem lie within the child in the same way that a child can have a disease or did the problem lie in the interactions between the child and the significant adult? Gillham, (1978), believed it to be in the interactions and thought that there was a problem in matching the view of hypnosis which was seen to only deal with the persons internal perception. However, a new, ecosystemic approach, linked hypnosis to the interactions of its subjects and was introduced by Fourie and de Beer (Fourie and de Beer, 1986). I happen to agree that the interaction of students with adults is the main cause of the behaviour problems that manifest themselves within schools and this is what should be addressed. It is true that many of these interactions happen outside of school and even before they ever attended your class but the power to make an impact on them still remains.

This is similar to a theory within neuro-linguistic programming (NLP) in which misunderstandings and conflict happen when one person's internal (perceived) map is significantly different from another's (Bradbury 2006, Freeman, 1999, Grinder, 1991). The idea of internal maps used by the founders of NLP, Richard Bandler and John Grinder, is taken from the book Manhood of Humanity (Korzbski, 1950) on general semantics; it states that a person's internal map starts being created when they begin to have an impact of the world around them, typically around 3-4 months old, and that this internal map is only a representation of their experiences. You will be able to draw parallels with the previous chapters that show that the world you build in your mind is just a representation of what you have experienced and what you expect.

This theory is used in NLP to signify that individual people do not, in general, have access to absolute knowledge of reality, but in fact only have access to a set of beliefs they have built up over time about reality. When two people have a different internal map of a current situation, misunderstandings occur and conflict ensues. Differences in maps generally occur when past experiences have been very different or when the amount of experience is significantly diverse. This can often occur between students and teachers who have vast differences in both the number and type of experiences to date. However, they also use the phrase, 'the map is not the terrain' to try and help people understand that whatever picture of the world they may hold in their minds, does not necessarily translate into the real world and therefore, there may be a need to change any preconceived ideas.

In NLP, a structured cluster of preconceived ideas and organized patterns of behaviours that are associated with certain places and people is known as a Schema (Piaget, 1928). The schema a student may have in one lesson could be very different to other classrooms or teachers within the same school. You may even have had a conversation about a student with another teacher where they are misbehaving in one class but a total angel in another. In fact, there are potentially hundreds of schemas, or set behaviour patterns, in your mind to cope with the variety of situations you find yourself in. This is a useful shortcut the brain has of creating behaviours suitable for different social situations which also aid it in adapting to new environments. Remember the analogy of you out with your friends versus going to see the queen.

What these internal maps and associated schemas tell us is that everyone, and I mean everyone, builds from just after birth, a working model of what the world is that is playing out in front of them. It does to ensure two things; that the world makes sense and that you are not going to be killed. However, recent analysis of brain makeup and adaptability has shown that human brains are remarkably elastic in their connections and will change and adapt, sometimes on a massive scale, in order to remain functional with relevant. There have been studies on patients that have suffered severe head trauma and even huge loss of brain tissue which show that the brain will re-route neural connections and re-assign roles to completely different areas of the brain to remain functional. Perhaps this flexibility has something to do with the way our brains are wired (or more accurately, not wired) from birth.

Take an animal for example, let's say a giraffe. When it is born it is able instantly able to hold its head up and within an hour can walk. If you compare this to human babies, how freaked out would a parent be if the same happened to their little baby? The reason that this doesn't happen in a human child is twofold. Firstly, the brain has grown to such a size that the head that contains it would not be able to fit down the mother's birth canal if it gestated any longer. So human babies are born severely premature to make sure it can fit down and can be born. Secondly, the vast majority of the 100 billion neurons or so that make up the brain are not connected, which means that there are hardly any behaviours set. It's not until the baby starts to interact with the world that the neurons start to make connections and the world around it starts to be painted (and therefore the subsequent required behaviours learnt).

As an example, let us pick up a family of naked mole rats with a newly born pup from Africa, and plonk it down in the arctic-circle. Now, what will the naked mole rat family do? Will it adapt to survive or be unable to unlearn its natural behaviour and die relatively quickly? If they do not, will the pup do anything different to what its parents have done? It will naturally want to dig, but when it finds snow instead of dirt, will it change its behaviour? Now do the same with a human family. Pick them up from a farm on the equator and plank them in the same place. Will they continue to walk around in shorts and t-shirt, basking in the sun, or will their behaviour change? Will the newly born child's behaviour be any different from their parents when they were the same age?

This is an over generalisation, but it highlights the remarkably ability of rapid and adaptable change that can occur in the human mind.

# UNDERSTANDING LANGUAGE EFFECTS

Here is a great example of how language can affect behaviour. Clasp your hands together but leave your index fingers outstretched and a couple of centimetres apart. Now look at the gap in between your fingers and say in your head the word 'close'. Say it over and over as loud as you can. What happens? Your fingers close right?

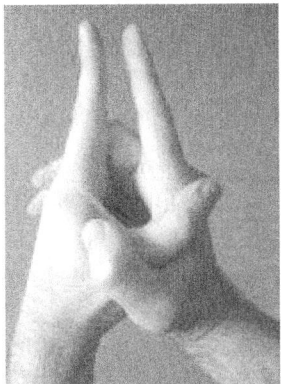

Image 10

Within the brain you are setting up a command, to close the gap, which is sent to your pre-motor cortex in order to prepare it to move. This in turn sets up tiny movements in anticipation of the movement which sets off a chain reaction that starts to obey your command. This is called an ideomotor affect. The same thing is happening when you hold a pendulum and imagine in rotating in a clockwise circle. The signal to prepare the motion will be sent and you muscles will fire in anticipation. This will cause an almost imperceptible movement which will start to make the pendulum swing.

Cortical hypotheses are created when the outgoing motor command signal (to close the gap) is sent from the motor cortex to the spinal cord and muscles. Simultaneously the same signal is transmitted back to the sensory and intermediate areas of the cortex, particularly the parietal lobe which maintains the body's position in space. This sequence of creating movement and behaviour from language can become automatic if done often enough or it is of specific value to the person. As the language driven behaviour is embedded, the control of the motor commands and behavioural responses move from the pre-frontal cortex to the posterior parietal cortex as already discussed. This has the effect of making the behaviour automatic and happens without the person being aware of it consciously. Therefore, the words that you use to elicit the behaviour you want become hard wired and automatic.

Language has a remarkable effect of our brains, more than we would actually suspect. The brain naturally seeks out and preserves patterns whether they come in the form of pictures, words or feelings and will attempt to make sense of them within the situation you are in. Your brain is filtering this information constantly so that your conscious mind can be free to focus on the task at hand and keep a consistent picture of the world. This means that when you are in the presence of someone else, whether you are talking or not, you are communicating with their subconscious, whether they know it or not.

A good example of when your subconscious filter alerts your conscious mind is when it hears something it deems important. The examples from the previous chapters on hearing your name in a crowded room, or words that are linked with danger show how your subconscious is taking in all the inputs (as limited as they are) from your senses and filtering them through your anterior cingulate gyrus, to monitor the environment for your safety. So, when your name is picked up, your subconscious determines that it is an important enough piece of information to be put above the threshold of awareness and alerts your conscious mind. The same applies for words or items that you put on The List. This means that a vast majority of words go underneath the radar of consciousness and go straight to the subconscious mind. Therefore, if the words you use are designed to talk directly to the subconscious, the mind isn't even aware of them.

With this in mind it would be good to look at what specific language and persuasion techniques there are and what they can do. This is not an exhaustive list, but it covers what we will be using in this book.

**Anchoring** is when you are given a point of reference (whether real of made up) that is linked to another piece of information. Do this exercise as an example. In Bristol, do you think there are more or less than 2 million people living? If you chose more or less, what figure would you put on it? We have anchored the Population of the city (Bristol) to a number (2 million). Chances are your guess wasn't too far away from that initial number. The actual answer is just over four hundred thousand, so even close. It works particularly well with numbers but can also be applied to real life. Here's another exercise to try.

'John is a happy and creative boy. He enjoys getting attention and being part of the popular crowd and especially enjoys attending regular dances. Although while he was at school he was a little self-obsessed he really enjoyed the opportunity of presenting and showing off in front of an audience'. Now take a look at these statements and choose one that is most likely. 1. John is a lawyer; 2. John is a professional actor; 3. John enjoys pop concerts; 4. John is a professional actor who enjoys pop concerts.

Did you decide that John was an actor more than a lawyer? Why? There are far more lawyers than there are professional actors so the odds are not in your favour. Can't lawyers be good speakers, be creative and enjoy dancing? As the description fitted your idea of what a 'typical' actor might have as his background, you were blinded into making a sensible estimation. Did you choose option four over option three? Why? Why would it be more likely that John enjoys pop concerts and is an actor? John could do anything as a job with the probability of him also liking a particularly type of concert even less likely. Anchoring is also used in hypnosis and NLP to link together a feeling, emotion, action or memory to a cue or trigger. It can also link behaviour and sound or smell which can then be used as a trigger to elicit the behaviour response on command.

**Availability Bias** happens when the perceived value of an object is increased when its availability is limited. You only have to look at anything that is 'limited edition' within clothing, jewellery or art, to see how much the price goes up because of it. The same happens with many other things. For example, you can set a task (such as a worksheet) that your class needs to do, however, you know the class will probably complain and moan. If you offer it with limited availability for certain people within the class, it suddenly becomes 'unfair' for the rest not to have one too, whereby you can look around and manage to find a few rarer sheets in another colour just for them.

**Representativeness** is the idea that when asked to judge how likely it is that A belongs to category B, people (or rather their automatic system) answer by asking how similar A is to their current stereotype of B. For example, what profession would think that a 6-foot-8-inch African-American man is more likely to have? 1 - A professional basketball player, 2 - A Barrister or 3 - A secretary? Your automatic system searches for the most common association between the two and will more than likely come up with answer A, simply because you know or have heard of more

6-foor-8-inch African-American basketball players than the others. This is similar to setting up an anchor except that the link has already been established within your own expectations. Another example with expectations is to imagine you have a coin and flip five heads in a row, what do you think the next result will be? Most people will say tails, as it is unlikely to flip six heads in a row when in fact there is still an equal chance of a head being flipped. This is where expectation and prior experience can influence choices.

**Status Quo Bias** was dubbed so by William Samuelson and Richard Zeckhauser in 1988. Humans are creatures of habit and will continue to do the same as they have done before in most situations. The main reasons for this is that, if we had to do something before and nothing bad has happened, we know it is relatively safe to continue to do it the same way. Our brains want to conserve energy so will prefer not to use its prefrontal cortex to consider the choices every time you do the same task. Most teachers know that students will sit in the same place every lesson, even without a seating plan, and will claim that someone is sitting in 'their' seat even if no allocations have been made. You may even find yourself doing the same in the cafeteria. Similarly, there are our own favourite spots on the sofa or in the dining room or our side of the bed that we instinctively want to inhabit every time.

Where the status quo bias really makes a difference is in relation to other people. We seldom want to stand out of the crowd where we might feel embarrassed or judged, and when we do want to, we usually follow another crowd in order to do so. Take the example of boys' wearing their shirts untucked in school. Many of the older, cooler kids do it so in order to fit in with them (and also not fit in with school) they comply with their status quo.

**Framing or frames** are devices for seeing the world a particular way. Which national newspaper you choose to read for instance, will report the events and topics with their own particular bias which will likely be a close match to your own frame of the world. A news story can be reported from many different angles but will only be published if the angle fits the papers' own frame. When frames are used to give people information it can be very powerful, for example, suppose you had a serious heart complaint and that your doctor suggests a very long and painful operation. You want to know the odds of surviving an operation like that and he tells you that out of a hundred patients who have had this operation, ninety are still alive five years later. What would you do? But what if instead the doctor told you that out of a hundred patients that have had this operation, ten are dead after five years. Doesn't sound that promising now does it? Framing a piece of information can make the difference between the choice you want being taken and not.

**Temptation & Mindlessness** are the Mr. Hyde of a person's personality. When in a calm or 'cold' state, a person can plan their future paths and make rational decisions such as going on a diet or not to punch another kid in the face when provoked. However, when something happens to put them in an aroused or 'hot' state, all the planning goes out of the window and the mere smell of a chip shop will have them buying a fish supper or swinging their fists away in a classroom. This is the difference between the planner in you (reflective) and the doer (automatic). This is often seen in students who can sit down and make plans for controlling their behaviour yet when they become aroused, those plans are worthless. This is why targets are used in schools, not just to focus on the positive behaviours wanted, but to increase the neural pathways of the behaviours you want so that they are more easily accessed when in a hot state. However, how often do those targets truly succeed? It is not always the student's fault however, as blood flow into the areas of higher function and control is reduced during arousal, making it difficult for any rational thinking to take place. This is why an imbedded, learned pattern of behaviour that is different from the emotional response is so important to set up.

An experiment was carried out involving shopaholics whereby at the start of the month, when in a calm and controlled state, they were given a special credit card that allowed them to set limits on their budgets. They could allocate so much for groceries, so much for entertainment and so much for clothes etc. This meant that when they walked past a window and were aroused by the new pair of shoes or the latest phone, they were no able to purchase it as the card would be declined. This worked so well in fact that the credit card company cancelled the experiment (probably due to the worry that it would lose so much money of people were not allowed to impulse buy and go into debt). This shows that we are able to put safety measures into place for whenever Mr Hyde came out to play, but they have to be effective and not rely on decisions made whilst in that state.

**Social Influences** come in two basic categories. The first on is information. If lots of people do something or think something, their actions and thoughts convey information about what might be best for you to do or think. An example of this would be if you were in a supermarket and you had two types of the same cheese to buy. On one shelf a certain brand has nearly sold out and on another shelf, it has hardly been touched. You are more likely to pick up the cheese that has almost gone because your subconscious is telling you that if other people bought that one it must be better (there is also some availability bias creeping in). That is also why restaurants sit customers in the window first, so that people outside can see that people have chosen to come in and eat so they are more likely to do the same. Would you enter a restaurant that is empty?

The second one is peer pressure. If you care about what certain people think about you then you are more likely to go along with the crowd to avoid their wrath or curry favour. Examples of this can be seen throughout schools and societies. You only have to look on social media to see a new wave of 'influencers' who give their opinion of products, games and fashion whose followers are likely to go out and buy what is recommended. This is why companies sponsor these people and ply them with free products.

**Priming** refers to how subtle cues can influence the brains automatic system into bringing certain information or behaviours to mind. Following research of this in supermarkets it has been shown that the mere fact that someone may ask you if you are likely to buy a certain product or not will bring to mind the thought of buying that product and a likely purchase of it. This is different from the 'free sample' demonstrators who work on the reciprocation expectation (if I give you something, it is expected that you will give me something back i.e. buy the product). Priming can influence behaviour from seemingly unrelated cues such as the image of a briefcase and boardroom table will make people less cooperative and less generous (Kat et al 2004). Setting up a prime as a trigger for language scripts is a great shortcut to use once they have been established and will get the students' subconscious ready for what follows.

**Feedback** is the best way to help people improve their performance and behaviour and a well-designed system can tell someone when they are doing well or when they are making a mistake. The best system however, provides feedback on when mistakes are about to happen so that they can be avoided. Consider your laptop computer suddenly closing down due to an unexpected error in the system. Wouldn't it have been better for the computer to detect the error and give you a two-minute warning of the shutdown so you can save you work? The closer the feedback is to the actions taken significantly improve their effect as the brain will link the two together more readily. This means that the closer an action is towards a student who is using unsuitable words in your lesson, the more likely they are to link the two together and understand your meaning. So the next time you suspect them of going to use the same language, you can use the same action to prevent it.

Another way that feedback can be used is in reducing emotional states. When you are with someone who is upset or angry, everything is a superlative. 'I hate them', 'it was the worst' etc. When speaking to them, it is possible to reduce their emotional state by feeding back what they are saying with a slight change to the words used. For example, 'I really hate that teacher', becomes, 'so you are not happy with them at the moment'. 'I had the worst lesson ever', becomes 'so you didn't have a good lesson today'. By reducing the emotional level of the feedback, you will begin to reduce not only the person's current emotional state but also their memory of it in the future. You are agreeing with their experience but using words that carry much less emotional attachment. This will help with their prediction of the next lesson.

It is also important to note that when you put a time limit on the feedback response, 'at the moment', 'today'; you are also letting them know that the state they are in is only temporary.

**Indirect association focusing** happens when you want to raise a matter without directing it in an obvious manner at the subject. A simple example of this would be talking about your mother when you want the subject to share things about their mother. It is a good example of leading a conversation onto subject matters you want raised. A master of this was the famous American psychiatrist Milton Erikson who would tell stories of his life in order for his patients to focus on the relevant issues in theirs. There is a whole genre of hypnosis based on his work known as Ericksonian Hypnosis.

**Binds & Double Binds** offer a choice in which either option will elicit the desired response. A bind pattern links an action to a feeling, the more you X the more you Y. For example 'the more you watch, the more curious you'll become' or 'the more you think about it, the more interesting you find it'. This is a basic persuasion technique that can be used to elicit a wanted response from a current action.
A double bind is a free choice between two outcomes, both of which will elicit a positive response. A parent's favourite example of this is 'you've had a really good day Harry, you can decide if you want to go to bed at 8 or 8:30'. The response wanted is little Harry to be in bed by 8:30 but, if you were to tell him to go to bed at 8:30 directly, he may well try to argue the case for a later time. Other examples of this are, 'would you like to pay with a card or cash?' (I want you to pay your bill now) or, 'would you like the injection in your arm or hip?' (You are going to get the jab one way or another)!

**Pacing & Leading** is a way of feeding back to subjects the experience they are having and then introducing them to a new desired behaviour – as you X so you Y; X being something you know to be true (such as them sitting, breathing, listening) and Y being the behaviour you want to elicit. Behaviour Y becomes connected with behaviour X as if they are interdependent. Using several pieces of X before a Y will create a stronger connection. For example, 'as you're reading these words you begin to feel your eyes getting heavier', or 'as you're reading these words, hearing the voice in your head, sitting in that chair, you begin to feel your eyes getting heavier'.

This is also setting up a 'yes' pattern response in the subject's mind. Yes, I am reading those words, yes, I am hearing the voice in my head, yes, I am sat in this chair, yes, my eyes are starting to get heavy.

**Presuppositions** hide the instructions you want the subject to pick up on by presupposing them to be the case already. It presupposes that the subject will do something or feel something even though you have not told them to do so explicitly. An example of this is, 'let me take your coat' presupposes that the person is going to stay and probably take a seat. Other examples are, 'don't forget your coat' (direction to leave), 'let me move your chair back' (direction to sit down). Presuppositions are also great when giving feedback on emotive states, (see Feedback).

**Tone of voice** can be as important as the words you use. Where possible it should be gentle and relaxed with phrases that flow easily. Practicing the script you write is important so that they it doesn't seem forced or unnatural. The tone of your voice can also be anchored to other meanings and phrases in order to bond them together. An example of this is to use the same tone of decreasing pitch in delivering the script as you do when giving a countdown.

Deepening of a trance is used to access a lower part of the subconscious mind in order to embed suggestions and links more firmly. Often in hypnosis, there is a deepening of the trance state by making the patient imagine that they are going down a stairwell or using a countdown of numbers to aid the induction. This is related to the image of going down or lowering yourself can be used to imbed the commands given. By using a simple countdown or by lowering the pitch of your voice you will accomplish the same result and by bringing your voice from a higher tone to a lower tone whilst also counting down produces a more pronounced sense of deepening.

**Imagery** is used to create an overall picture or feel of what you are saying and it should appeal to all the senses. A multi-sensory approach to the words you use will deepen the link with the subjects' brain and the actions required. For example, if I told you to think of a beach, you could probably do that. If, however, I told you to think of a beach, to see the waves crashing on the shore, to hear the sound it makes as it does so, so taste the salty air and feel the cool breeze blowing over your skin, you are much more likely to be put into a frame of mind where you are actually there.

# HOW TO WRITE A SCRIPT

Example

As you know, humans are constantly making predictions about the world around them based on their experiences and expectations of how the world is likely to be in the near future in part from their knowledge of what their actions have been in the past (Taylor, 2004). So the first thing we set up in planning a script is a prime and trigger that will allow the mind to predict the script that will follow. This should mean that the prime, trigger and the script will become so closely linked that by just using them the prime and trigger, the script will run unconsciously without you having to say it out loud every time. It's the same as the end of one song on an album is a prime for the next one that you will instantly start to sing even if it doesn't come on.

What I do then is to add a pacing and leading phrase using five elements which also sets up a 'yes' response in the mind. I make sure my tone of voice starts higher and lowers in tone as I speak it. I then deepen these commands by counting down from 5 (the same number used in the pacing and leading) using the same lowering tone.

Once the behaviour I have asked for has been shown I reward them with praise (releasing a good shot of dopamine) and also use the trigger again to link it the pleasant feeling.

Here is an example script that I have used:

Handclap – Prime
'Listen' – Trigger
'As you sit there, talking to your friends, listening to my voice, I want you to turn around and focus on me' – pacing and leading
'5, 4, 3, 2, 1' – deepening
'That's great, well done' with hand clap – praise and link to prime

I set up a prime by using the sound of a hand clap. This is a signal to the subconscious that something is coming that it should pay attention to. By also having it linked to the praise and dopamine release at the end of the script makes the mind anticipate the good feeling to come.

Then the word 'listen' is used as the trigger, which then sets up the script running. Just like the words of the next album track, their subconscious predicting what is to follow. This may take several uses of the full script to embed and then to be used occasional use after that to ensure a firm connection.

The first two comments in the main section of the script of 'sitting there' and 'talking to your friends' are confirmed subconsciously while the third comment of 'listening to my voice' not only confirms what they are doing but will increase their focus on it. The fourth and fifth comments tell them the behaviour that is desired which continues to be accepted along with the first three comments by setting up a yes pattern. So in the mind it looks like:

'As you sit there' – yes I'm sat here
'Talking to your friends' – yes I'm talking to my friends
'Listening to my voice' – yes I can hear your voice
'I want you to turn around' – yes I will turn around
'And listen to me' – yes I will listen to you

Other behaviours could be inputted in place of the last two comments to use in different scenarios if you wanted to redirect attention or focus students on a different task or if you wanted to give other commands such as packing away or clearing up. The first set of comments should be things that the students are doing that will set up a yes pattern.

The deepening stage of the script is a count down from five to zero. This has two uses. Firstly, it gives the student time to assimilate what the command has been and will also give a clear timeline of compliance. Secondly, it serves to deepen the commands in the pacing & leading section.

Finally, the praise stage is linked to a positive emotional feeling and release of dopamine with the completion of the task. An example of the praise is, "That's great, well done" followed by the prime sound of the hand clap. This links the clap to the positive feeling of praise making the use of the prime at the start of the script more powerful.

Breaking the script down into its component parts will help you to input different sections according to the scenario you wanted to use it in.

One of the comments made by my colleagues after I had taught them how to use this script showed an interesting effect. They said that the students whom the script most directly applied to, (those that were not facing the teacher and were talking to their friends) responded better than those who were already doing what was being asked. A reason for this could be that the script uses pacing and leading of what the student is doing to set up a positive 'yes' response in their minds. This is then linked to the desired behaviour before being imbedded deeper with a countdown. If the students are not talking to their friends or facing away from the teacher, the pacing and leading would not set up this 'yes' response and so not be firmly linked to the desired behaviour. Similarly, if the pacing and leading matched the students' behaviour exactly it will have a stronger effect. This means that it could be used to focus the request on particular students in a class making it a more specific tool.

There is a danger, however, in having a tool that can be this specific and responsive. The purpose of this book is to teach you how to use specific language scripts and techniques that can be used to decrease negative behavioural responses and increase positive relationships with students. Although the purposes of the scripts are for positive outcomes it would not be difficult to extrapolate their use to include other behavioural areas that could be influenced. This may include negative uses of the script to influence choices, friendships and behaviour. Whether each use of the script would influence in a positive way needs to be examined carefully before you use it.

By using the practice script sheets, you will begin to be able to examine what it is you are trying to achieve and how you will put the script together.

**Class Detail** – In this section fill with a description of the class as a whole and decide if all or some of the class is to be targeted for the scripts use. This will help you select relevant pacing messages to use and age appropriate language.

**Purpose** – The purpose of the script should be examined closely as to what it is you want the script to do exactly. The more specific you are, the better the script will be. Is it for getting attention, for ease movement around the class or to keep students from getting out of their seats?

**Prime** – What you are going to use to get the students ready for the script? It should be short and sharp and be able to be used with the 'praise' section.

**Trigger** – This is the start of the script and will be used to automatically run it once established.

**Main Section** – Where you can build up the pacing & leading language, the presuppositions or binds that you want to give. You will also set out what behaviours you want to elicit from your students here in short focused phrases.

**Deepening** – What is the most relevant deepening technique required?

**Praise** – How are you going to praise the right behaviour? It should be as natural as possible.

# SCRIPT SHEET

| Class detail |
| --- |
| **Purpose** |
| **Prime** |
| **Trigger** |
| **Main section** |
| **Deepening** |
| **Review** |

# SCRIPT SHEET - EXAMPLE

**Class detail** – Year 10, mixed ability and mixed sex. The section of the class I want to focus on are boys.

**Purpose** – To focus on a section of the class that sits at the back and talk over me when I give instructions. I want them to stop talking and focus on me

**Prime** – Bang on desk

**Trigger** - Ready

**Main section** – use pacing and leading to set up a yes pattern

As you sit there,

talking to your friends,

listening to my voice,

I want you to turn around

and focus on me

**Deepening** – Use a countdown

   5, 4, 3, 2, 1

**Review** – The Prime of banging on the desk didn't feel right so will switch it to a hand clap. I have decided to change the Trigger to more of a direct command so will now use the word Listen.

Using just the Prime and Trigger alone is not as good on a Monday as they have forgotten the script. So every Monday I will use the script as a whole and drop it down to just the Prime and Trigger after that.

# SCRIPTS

As you can see, writing a behaviour language script is relatively straightforward. Simply layout what you want to accomplish and what words/phrases you are going to use in each section.

The review section at the bottom of the sheet is just as important as the rest. This is where you get to reflect on the script and its impact in order to make changes and adapt to better suit you and your students. There is a mix and match language bank at the end of this section with examples of words and phrases to use. You will notice that is has plenty of space to add your own so please do.

The knowledge and language patterns in this book can offer much more than just the scripts. It can also help you use this information when working with individual students, small group and even whole schools. Following the mix and match word bank are examples of how this can be done. They include looking specifically at using language and anchors to tie behaviours together.

It will also look at memes and their uses and help you think about and structure your ideas in three specific ways. What is important, is that you understand what you want from each element and what you can use to make it so

# MIX AND MATCH
# LANGUAGE BANK

## PRESUPPOSITIONS

| Purpose | Presupposition |
|---------|----------------|
| Sit down | As they come in – 'Don't forget to put your bag under your seat' |
| Stand up | Mind the table behind you as you get up |
| Leave the room | Thanks everyone, see you next time |
| Do the work | That's coming along really well and will look great when it's finished |

# PACING AND LEADING

| Pacing | Leading | Optional | Desired Behaviour |
|---|---|---|---|
| As you sit in your seat | I want you to | Automatically | Turn around |
| | You will | Instinctively | Stop talking |
| As you're listening to my voice | You'll want to | Unconsciously | Stop what you're doing |
| | You choose to | Involuntarily | Open you're books |
| As you're talking to your friends | You feel compelled to | Spontaneously | Focus on me |
| As you sit at your desk | | Without thinking | Face forward |
| As you breath in and out | | | |

# ANCHORS

| Behaviour wanted | Anchor | Use |
|---|---|---|
| Answering questions in class | Double knock on the table | Double tap directly after anyone answers a question to set up the link between answering and knocking. Use the knock to elicit answers when none are forthcoming |
| Follow agreed behaviour plan | Red dot on paper | Red dot on paper on the wall on my room where the plan was set up. Red dot on the wall of the classroom to link the two. |

# PRIMES AND TRIGGERS

| Vocal | Noise |
|---|---|
| Listen | Hand clap |
| Ready | Table knock |
| Focus | Finger click |
| Stop | Buzzer |
| Look | |

# FRAMES

| Desired frame | Framing |
|---|---|
| Feel good about choosing to stay in | Of course you can go out in the cold tonight. I'll be here with the heating on watching... |
| Feel like taking an airplane is safe | The odds of the plane crashing are 1 in 11 million |

# BINDS AND DOUBLE BINDS

| Purpose | Bind | Double bind |
|---|---|---|
| Go to bed | The more you watch tv, the more tired you become | Would you like to go to bed at 8 or 8:30 tonight? |
| Sign up for after school club | The more you think about it the more you'll want to sign up | Do you want to sign up with my pen or my pencil? |
| Take your coat off | As you sit there you'll notice it getting hotter and hotter | Would you like to hang your coat on the back of your chair or put it away in your bag? |

# DEEPENING

Count down

Lowering of tone

Lowering of hand

'Deeper'

'Going down'

'Sinking'

# LANGUAGE PLAN

**Details**

**Purpose**

**Main**

**Review**

# LANGUAGE PLAN – EXAMPLE 1

**Details** – Class of 25, year 8, low/middle set, a number of students from my tutor group

**Purpose** – Two students from my tutor group and are having trouble keeping to their behaviour targets. I need them to remember what we talked about and agreed during our meetings without making reference to them out loud to the class.

**Main** – During the 1:1 sessions I will place a large red dot on a piece of paper within eye sight of the student, perhaps higher and to the right. I will make no reference to it. We will agree targets and discuss behaviour and feelings when in the class.

I will put a copy of the red dot in front of the classroom to anchor desired behaviour target to the classroom setting.

**Review** – The first week was a slight improvement but needs more 1:1 work.

I have increased the size of the red dot in the classroom in order to increase the emphasis.

I have also used a red board pen to mark a dot on the board when I begin to feel behaviour slipping.

# LANGUAGE PLAN – EXAMPLE 2

**Details** - Class of 30, year 10, low set. I am supporting a student 1:1 who has difficulties in talking in class and responding appropriately to instructions.

**Purpose** - I want the student I am supporting to model the good behaviour of certain students in the class so that they are able to make appropriate responses to the teacher.

**Main** - While I am sat next to the student I will attempt to anchor the good behaviour of others in the class to a sound that I create. I will then use this anchor to elicit the correct responses to questions and instructions the student gets from the teacher.

I will use a double tap either on the table, on my leg or on the student themselves to anchor the good behaviour.

I will then use the double knock when the student is asked a question or given instructions by the teacher.

**Review** - The embedding of the anchor took longer than I thought. It only works sometimes and needs to be embedded deeper. I will use the same anchor when praise is given.

It is working much better. I use it every time a good behaviour is shown in the lesson and also to elicit the same response from my student. I use it when praise is given for the good response as well.

I am finding I have to use the trigger less and less and the student is finding their feet in responding to the teacher. I will continue to monitor.

# CREATE YOUR OWN MEME

In order to create your own meme you must first think hard about what it is you are trying to accomplish because once you set it free, it may take on a life of its own! That being said, it is possible to set up the meme with specific focus and direction that will, at some level, limit its mutation.

As described, there are three main ways to set up and distribute a meme; The Trojan Horse, Repetition and Cognitive Dissonance. Each one will have benefits over the other depending on the meme, the situation it will be used in and the purpose it is to fulfil.

The Trojan Horse method of infecting a mind is best done when the meme is activity based over time. In this way the person gets tied deeper into the meme the more time and effort they spend on it. If they are involved in spreading the message of this meme this will tie them in even more and if challenged on it, a cognitive dissonance will form that will make them defend the meme, regardless of what the memeplex is now unpacking.

Repetition Is best used when a simple meme is needing to be introduced or reinforced. This can be seen in use in a countries' national anthem, a school's motto, or a TV show's catchphrase. It is best done in numerous formats such as an image, phrase and music.

A cognitive dissonance is a little more of a complex thing to set up. After you establish what meme you want them to be infected with, you then have to find out what of their current views can be used. You then have to present a conflicting message that produces a large enough gap. Only then will you be able to offer the meme you want taken up as a bridge between the two.

There are some planning sheets and examples for you to use and see how they can be set up.

# MEME PLAN – TROJAN HORSE

**Purpose of meme:**

**Describe the meme:**

**Language of the meme:**

**Colours of the meme:**

**Associated memes:**

**Face meme:**

**How will it spread:**

# MEME PLAN – TROJAN HORSE

**Purpose of meme:**

Change the school's expectation images and key phrases

**Describe the meme:**

The schools expectations are Teamwork, Sustainability and Respect. Key phrases for each will be We achieve more together (Teamwork), We are responsible to make things better (Sustainability) and We look out for each other (Respect)

**Language of the meme:**

Inclusive, together, as one, improve, sustain, look after, stand up, maintain, support, uphold, nurture, value, admire

**Colours of the meme:**

Blue, image of hand helping another up (Teamwork), Green, image of hands on tools (Sustainability) Yellow, image of hand around shoulders (Respect)

**Associated memes:**

School cleanliness, respect for building, respect for each other, respect for environment, friendship, team-spirit, inclusion, achievement, peer-support, friendly competition, encouragement

**Face meme:**

'Our School'

**How will it spread:**

School logo, Individual images for each expectation, competitions, assemblies, teachers' language, linked rewards

# MEME PLAN – REPETITION

| Purpose of meme: |
| :--- |
| |
| **Describe the meme:** |
| |
| **Language of the meme:** |
| |
| **Colours of the meme:** |
| |
| **1st way of showing meme:** |
| |
| **2nd way of showing meme:** |
| |
| **3rd way of showing meme:** |
| |
| **How will it spread:** |
| |

# MEME PLAN – REPETITION EXAMPLE

**Purpose of meme:**

Persuade my year 10 class to choose to make a picnic bench when given the choice of topics.

**Describe the meme:**

Thoughts of a picnic bench in their mind, a clear shape of the structure.

**Language of the meme:**

Bench, Picnic, Flat top, Table, Outdoors, Seating.

**Colours of the meme:**

Wood, Brown, Blue picnic logo

**1st way of showing meme:**

Images of picnic bench in places where the group pass.

**2nd way of showing meme:**

Use keywords when talking to the group.

**3rd way of showing meme:**

Tell story of a recent picnic

**How will it spread:**

No intention to spread outside of the group

# MEME PLAN – COGNITIVE DISSONANCE

| |
|---|
| **Purpose of meme:** |
| **Describe the meme:** |
| **Language of the meme:** |
| **Colours of the meme:** |
| **Current meme:** |
| **Dissonance meme:** |
| **Bridge meme:** |
| **How will it spread:** |

# MEME PLAN – COGNITIVE DISSONANCE EXAMPLE

| |
|---|
| **Purpose of meme:** |
| To get students to choose to take History at year 9 GCSE options |
| **Describe the meme:** |
| Set up a new subject name 'Forensic History', connotations to CSI TV shows and Forensic Science |
| **Language of the meme:** |
| Crime Scene Investigation, Forensic History, Exciting Investigations, Murder |
| **Colours of the meme:** |
| Yellow & Black (crime scene tape), Blue, White |
| **Current meme:** |
| History is a boring subject |
| **Dissonance meme:** |
| You should choose to take History as a GCSE option |
| **Bridge meme:** |
| Choosing Forensic History is not choosing boring history but a cool new subject |
| **How will it spread:** |
| Word of mouth through students by setting up fun, historical CSI events in their year 8 lessons a month before options |

# MEMETICS CONCLUSION

As you can see, there are huge links between the language of persuasion and the power of memetics. This could be due to the subconscious control systems of our mind being built with memes are very much influenced by the language inputs received.

Memes are everywhere you look from clothes, chairs, haircuts, houses, government and music. Everything around you is the result of an idea spreading and influencing people. Most of this is happening without you being aware of it. You could say that getting infected by memes is the whole purpose of the brain and that our thin veneer of consciousness is just along for the ride. This may be an uncomfortable truth that we'd simply rather ignore. Most of the memes that come our way have only a fleeting influence on our lives and are soon replaced by newer, stronger ones. The memes that stick are the ones that infect your brain deeply and seem to plug the biggest cognitive dissonance within a subconscious.

This large cognitive gap often occurs when a physical loss is experienced such as a death of a close friend or family member. It also occurs in highly negatively and positively charged situations where your limbic system (paleomammalian brain) is flooded with chemicals such as endorphin and adrenaline that create long lasting memories through the hippocampus, amygdala and limbic system. As a result, a person may start to believe all sorts of unusual ideas such as a dead relative is only in the next room, the government is conspiring to keep the truth about an event secret or that the good feelings you get when you are with someone you love will hide the uncomfortable feelings you may feel when they ask you to do something you don't want to.

When it comes to larger crowds however, the dynamic and influences change slightly. From a psychological point of view, a crowd can present wholly new characteristics that are very different from the individuals that compose it. Indeed, there have been many examples of this on a large scale including those from history such as Tulipomania, The South-Sea Bubble and the Mississippi Scheme right up to the more recent London riots. What is it that changes a singular person's behaviour when in a crowd is a fascinating subject and if you are interested, there are several great books that you can read on it in the Further Reading section.

# ABOUT THE AUTHOR

Tony Curtis is an award winning behaviour specialist who has been working in the educational setting for over 25 years. From Teaching Assistant to Assistant Principal, his focus has been on improving the behaviour and outcomes of students so that they can have successful, fulfilling lives. He has a degree in education and numerous diplomas in Cognitive Behaviour Therapy, Brief Solution Focused Therapy and Hypnotherapy. He has previously been a Royal Marine, a full contact Taekwondo champion and British coach, a photographer and Managing Director of several award winning businesses. He is currently competing in Team GB in the Pentathlon series and is a Gold and Silver international athlete.

# IMAGE AND BOOK REFERENCES & FURTHER READING

Image 1: Steven Saletta

Image 2: Bernard Dupont

Image 3: Images courtesy of www.neuroscientificallychallenged.com

Image 4: From Bradley & Petry, 1977

Image 5: Edward H Adelson, 2005

Image 6: Edward H Adelson, 2005

Image 7: Uri Paz

Image 8: Huzaifa Dulal

Image 9: Akiyoshi Kitaoka (Kitaoka and Ashida 2003)

Image 10: Richard Wiseman

Astor, M. (1971) Learning Through Hypnosis. The Education Forum

Ariely, D. (2009) Predictably Irrational: The hidden forces that shape our decisions. Harper Collins Publishers. The revised and expanded edition.

Benson, G. (1984) Short-Term Hypnotherapy with Delinquent and Acting-Out Adolescents. British Journal of Experimental and Clinical Hypnosis

Blackmore, S. (1999) The Meme Machine. Oxford University Press.

Bradbury, A. (2006) Develop Your NLP Skills. Kogan Page

Britannica. (2008) The Brain: A guided Tour of the Brain – Mind, Memory, and Intelligence. Robinson

Brodie, R. (1996) Virus of the mind. Integral Press. Seattle

Brown, D. (2006) Tricks of the Mind. Channel Four Books

Cialdini, R. (2007) Influence: The Psychology of Persuasion. Collins Business

Claxton, G. (2005) The Wayward Mind. Abacus Publishing

Collett, P. (2003) The Book of Tells. Bantam Books

Dale, R. A. (1972) Hypnosis and Education, Education Research information Centre Document Reproduction Service, ED 087 710

Dennet, D. C. (2003) Freedom Evolves. London: Allen Lane

Duffy, B. (2018) The perils of perception. Atlantic Books

Edelman, G, M. & Tononi, G. (2000) Consciousness: How matter becomes imagination

Fontana, D. (1985) Classroom control: understanding and guiding classroom behaviour. Volume 1 of Psychology in Action. British Psychological Society

Fourie, D. and de Beer, M. (1986) Hypnotic Analgesia: Some implications of a

Ecosystemic approach. British Journal of Experimental and Clinical Hypnosis

Gardner, H. and Seana, M. (2006). The science of Multiple Intelligences theory: A response to Lynn Waterhouse. Educational Psychologist, Volume 41, Issue 4, Fall 2006, pp. 227–232. 53

Gibson, M. (1984) Hypnosis with Children: A reply to Cowel' comments, British journal of Hypnosis, 2, 41-42

Gillham, W. (1978) Reconstructing Educational Psychology. Beckham: Croom Helm. USA

Greenfield, S. (2008) Id: The Quest for Meaning in the 21st Century. Hodder & Stroughton LTD

Grinder, M. (1991) The Educational Converyor Belt. Metamorphous Press. USA

Guadango, R. E. (2009) Are certain genders or body types better at the art of persuasion? Taken from Scientific American Mind. July

Halpern, D. (2015) Inside the nudge unit: How small changes can make a big difference. Ebury Publishing

Harris, S. (2012), Free Will. Free Press

Hartley, G. & Karinch, M. (2009) How to Spot a Liar. Crimson Publishing

Heap, M. (1988) Hypnosis: Current Clinical, Experimental and Forensic Practices. Croom Helm. USA

Kember, D., Leing, D. Y. P., Jones, A., Yuen Loke, A., Mckay, J., Sinclair, K., Tse, H., Webb, C., Wong, FKY., Wong, M. and Yeung, E. (2000). 'Development of a questionnaire to measure the level of reflective thinking', Assessment and Evaluation in Higher Education, 25 (4): 381-95

Korzybski, A. (1950) Manhood of Humanity, Institute of General Semantics, hardcover, 2nd edition

Le Bon, G. (1896) The Crowd: A study of the popular mind. Digireads.com Publishing

Lozanov, G. (1978) Suggestology and Outlines of Suggestopaedia. London: Gordon Breach

Lovat, T. J. (Ed.) (1992). Sociology for teachers. NSW: Social Science Press.

McNiff, J., Lomax, P. & Whitehead, J. (1996). You and your action research project. London: Routledge 54

Mackay, C. (1841) Extraordinary popular delusions and the madness of crowds. Harriman House Classics

MacMillan, P. W. (1988) The use of Hypnosis and Suggestopedia in Children with Learning Difficulties. From Heap. M (1998) Hypnosis – Current Clinical Experimental and Forensic practices. Croom Helm. Chapter 26

Martin, S & Darnley, L. (2004) The Teaching Voice, London: Whurr Publishing

Mezirow, J. (1990). How critical reflection triggers transformative learning. In Mezirow, J. & Associates, Fostering critical reflection in adulthood: A guide to transformative and emancipatory learning (pp.1-20). San Francisco: Jossey-Bass

Morgan, L. (2009). VAK Learning Styles. [Online] Availble from: http://articles.getacoder.com/Vark_Learning_Styles_517538x1143183909.htm

Neill, S. and Caswell, C. (2005) Body Language for Competent Teachers. Routledge. London

Norton, L. S. (2009). Action Research in Teaching & Learning, A Practical Guide to Conducting Pedagogical Research in Universities

Noffke, S. E. (1995). 'Action research and Democratic Schooling: Problematics and Potentials', in S. Noffke and R. B. Stvenson (eds), Educational Action Research: Becoming Practically Critical. New York: Teachers College Press. Pp. 1-10.

Norton, L. S. (2009). Action Research in Teaching & Learning, A Practical Guide to Conducting Pedagogical Research in Universities

Papadotas, S.P. (1973). Color them motivated-color's psychological effects on students. National Association of Secondary School Principals Bulletin, 57(370), 92-94.
Piaget, J. (1928). The Child's Conception of the World. London: Routledge and Kegan Paul

Pulvermuller, F. (2002) The Neuroscience of Language: On Brain Circuits of Words and Serial Order. Cambridge 55

Sinofsky, E.R. & Knirck, F.G. (1981). Choose the right color for your learning style. Instructional Innovator, 26(3), 17-19.

Taylor, K. (2004) Brainwashing: The Science of Thought Control. Oxford

Thaler, R. and Sunstein, C. (2009) Nudge: Improving decisions about health, wealth and happiness. Penguin Books

Wiseman, R. (2009) :59 seconds: Think a little, change a lot. Macmillan

Wiseman, R. (2007) Quirkology: The curious science of our everyday lives. Macmillan

Printed in Great Britain
by Amazon

21502110R00045